£1.99

KU-608-573

HOW TO SPEAK GOLF

Also by Sally Cook, with illustrations by Ross MacDonald

How to Speak Baseball:
An Illustrated Guide to Ballpark Banter

Special thanks to:
Bob Cook, Jill Hanekamp,
Chris Millard, and Judith Powell

HOW *to* SPEAK

SALLY COOK and ROSS MACDONALD

An Illustrated Guide to Links Lingo

FLATIRON
BOOKS

www.flatironbooks.com

The Library of Congress Cataloging-in-Publication data is available upon request.

ISBN 978-1-250-07197-2 (paper over board)
ISBN 978-1-250-07198-9 (e-book)

Designed by Mike Gmitter

Our books may be purchased in bulk for promotional, educational, or business use. Please contact your local bookseller or the Macmillan Corporate and Premium Sales Department at (800) 221-7945, extension 5442, or by e-mail at MacmillanSpecialMarkets@macmillan.com.

First Edition: May 2016

10 9 8 7 6 5 4 3 2 1

INTRODUCTION

The vernacular of golf, some of which is centuries old, conjures up powerful images of what's happening out on the course. Unlike many other sports, golf provides countless hours for players to actually talk to one another. Why say, "He's a poor player," when you can describe a guy who digs up the turf when he swings as a "hacker," a "duffer," or a "chopper"? How about when a player twitches when putting? Wouldn't it be more fun and expressive to declare, "She's got the 'yips,' the 'staggers,' the 'shakes,' the 'jitters,' the 'jerks,' or the 'flinches'"? And what player would say, "I hit the ball high and hard," when he could simply say, "Did you see my zinger?"

Ever since the very first games of golf were played in the mid-1400s, a plethora of lively links lingo has evolved along with a treasure trove of stories about the game. For instance, why is Mary Queen of Scots considered the Mother of Golf? Where in the world is the worst golf course? How important is fashion to the game? Which famous players are known as "Big Momma," "Slammin' Sammy," and "Boss of the Moss"? Here we've gathered some of our favorite golf terms and stories and paired them with illustrations that are just as colorful as the words. Whether you're a novice on the greens, a pro, or simply a fan, we think you'll relish learning and speaking a whole new language.

ARMY GOLF

APPROACH SHOT

A shot from the fairway with the goal of landing the ball on the green.

APRON

A ring of grass surrounding the green, shorter than the fairway but longer than the grass of the green. **Frog Hair. Fringe. Collar.**

ARMY GOLF

The inconsistent hitting of the ball from one side of the fairway to the other. Left, right, left. **Hitting Out of Both Barrels.**

AWAY

The player whose ball is farthest from the hole. He/she plays first.

BACKDOOR

When the ball hits the back edge of the cup and falls in the hole.

CLUBHOUSE CHATTER: GOLF'S ORIGINS

Golf, as we know the game, most likely emerged in Scotland. Though there is still debate regarding which country invented the sport, legend has it that a group of sheepherders grew bored tending to their flocks, not far from what is now the Saint Andrews Golf Club, one of the first. These shepherds whacked pebbles and stones into rabbit- and foxholes with their wooden "crooks" or staffs. Various versions of this game were played in nearly every area of the world, including China, Italy, France, Holland, Belgium and even Laos, long before Scotland claimed to invent the game.

The word "golf" originates from the Old Scots terms "glove" or "goff," having evolved from the medieval Dutch term "kolf," meaning "club." The Scots, using wooden balls from Holland, played their game on parkland, whereas the Dutch played a similar game on ice. By the early fifteenth century Scots were playing the game in its rudimentary form: swinging at a ball with a club in order to move it from start to finish with as few strokes as possible. The first documented mention of golf in Scotland was in a 1457 Act of the Scottish Parliament, an edict issued by Scottish King James II, banning the sport, because he thought it distracted soldiers from their archery practice. His son, James III, upheld the ban in 1471. Twenty years later his son, James IV, continued the ban once again until 1502 when the King himself became captivated with the sport and lifted the ban.

During Scotland's short peace with England in the early 1500s, the English, too, established golf. When Scotland and England went back to war in 1547 the game declined in England. But when James VI of Scotland took the throne in England in 1603 and became known as James I (from the union of the Scottish and English crowns), golf returned to England to stay. A group of Edinburgh players were the first to organize a golf club in 1744, and were the first to write rules for the game, easily familiar to modern-day golfers.

BACKSPIN

The reverse spinning of the ball causing it to slow down or roll back toward the player once it lands on the green. **Juice. Junk. English.**

BAILOUT

Purposely playing or aiming away from hazards or bunkers. No need to post a bond.

BALL MARK

A flat, dime-sized object. Marks the position of the ball on the green, when it lies between another ball and the hole.

BANANA BALL

Slice or shot that fades to the right (left to right for righties) in a banana-shaped curve. **Extreme Slice.** This shot has no appeal.

BARKY

Hitting a tree, but still getting a good score.

BARKY

CLUBHOUSE CHATTER: HELL HOLES

"Hazard" usually refers to features built into a golf course to make play more difficult, but the term takes on a new meaning at the Skukuza Golf Course in Kruger National Park, South Africa. Here, the hazards are mobile and unpredictable: lions, elephants, buffalo, leopards, and rhinos. When confronted by four-legged hazards, golfers are advised not to run, but to back away slowly… and forget about finishing the hole.

BLAST

BEST BALL

A favored form of match play in which the best ball (lowest score) of two players is pitted against the lowest score of the competing team.

BIRD DOG

The driving club. Golfers sometimes say "Time to let the big dog eat" when they decide to use the driver instead of a higher lofted and short club. Best when the dog makes no barky.

BIRDIE

Score of one under par on a given hole.

BLAST

A mighty swing of the club that deliberately scoops and strikes the sand just behind the ball to hit the ball out of a sand trap. **An Explosion.**

BOGEY

Score of one over par on a given hole.

CLUBHOUSE CHATTER: WORLD'S WORST GOLF COURSE?

Arguably, the course on Ascension Island, a speck
of land in the South Atlantic, a thousand miles
from the nearest continent, Africa, holds two golf
course superlatives: worst and most remote. With
no grass, the "greens," called "browns," are made
of crushed compacted lava and held together by
diesel oil. It's no wonder that Ascension Island's
own government's website labels it the worst in the
world. Most remote? Well, that's obvious.

BREAK

A putted ball's deviation from a straight path due to undulations in the surface of the green.

BUNKER

A fairway hazard in the form of a depression in the ground filled with sand. Derives from the Scottish word for scar. **Sand Trap. Cat Box. Kitty Litter. Beach.**

BURIED LIE

A ball that lands in a trap and is partially covered in sand. **A Fried Egg.**

CABBAGE

The worst of the rough. **Spinach. Lettuce.** A salad to be avoided.

BUNKER

CADDIE OR CADDY

CADDIE OR CADDY

Derives from the French "cadet," the person who carries a player's bag and clubs, and advises the player about the unique characteristics of the course.

CART GOLF

When two players sharing a cart hit their shots to a similar, easily reached location.

CASUAL WATER

A condition in which heavy rain or poor drainage has left a portion of fairway intentionally soggy. The player is entitled to relief.

CHECK

The outcome of backspin when the ball lands on the green. **Bite. Grab. Hold.**

CLUBHOUSE CHATTER: WORLD'S BIGGEST SAND BUNKER

The former course at the Aramco compound in Dhahran, Saudi Arabia, consisted of nothing but sand, making it one endless bunker. The sand, soaked in readily available oil and packed down, formed a smooth putting surface when dried. Did the die-hard golfers use a sand wedge on every shot? Actually, no…each golfer carried a piece of artificial turf for teeing up the ball. The course has since been replaced by a conventional grass course, to no one's disappointment.

CHEF

A player who can't stop slicing the ball. A real cutup!

CHICKEN STICK

Playing it safe by using a low-risk club for a tough shot.

CHILI DIP

Hitting the ground and digging up turf before hitting the ball, resulting in little or no contact with the ball itself. **Fat, Heavy,** or **Chunk Shot.**

CHIP

A shot meant to fly for a short time and then roll or bounce most of its way toward the hole.
Chip and Run. Chip and Roll.
Bump and Run.

CHILI DIP

CHOKE DOWN

CHOKE DOWN
Gripping farther down on the golf club. The opposite of "choking up," for example, on a baseball bat.

CLUB FACE
The flat, grooved surface of a clubhead, used for striking the ball.

CLUBHEAD SPEED
Measured in mph or kph, the speed of the club head, at the moment of impact with the ball. **Head Speed.**

COIL
Turning the shoulders and hips during the backswing before beginning the downswing.

DANCE FLOOR
The green. The putting surface. Not a swinging place.

CLUBHOUSE CHATTER: LOWEST 18-HOLE SCORE

The lowest score on a course of at least 6,500 yards in length is 55. Rhein Gibson, an Australian pro, shot it on May 12, 2012 at River Oaks Golf Club in Edmond, Oklahoma, an eighteen-hole, 6,850-yard par 71 course. Gibson parred the first hole, followed that with an eagle, a birdie, an eagle, and then five straight birdies for a 26 over his first nine holes. Then on his back nine he had two pars, then three birdies, a par, and three more birdies for a second nine of 29 and a total of 55. Just a week earlier Gibson had set the course record of 60. His 55 will likely be tough to beat.

DEWSWEEPERS

Players who prefer the earliest morning tee times.

DIMPLES

The round indentations on the ball, which give it lift. Balls have from 330-500 dimples.

DIVOT

The hunk of dirt and grass that is displaced when a player strikes the ball.

DOGLEG

A fairway that is straight for some distance and then bends to the left or the right, resembling the shape of a dog's leg. No hydrants along the way.

DOG TRACK

Derogatory term for a golf course in poor condition. **A Goat Track.**

DEWSWEEPERS

CLUBHOUSE CHATTER: HELL HOLES

Hole number 14 at the Coeur d'Alene Resort Golf Course in Idaho sports another unusual type of hazard. The green is located on a floating platform in a lake, the entire "fairway" a water hazard. Well-prepared golfers bring plenty of extra balls…preferably used ones.

DOUBLE BOGEY

DOUBLE BOGEY
Scoring two strokes above par on a hole.

DOUBLE EAGLE
Scoring three below par on any hole.

DRAIN
To sink a putt into the cup.

DRIVE
The initial shot on each hole, hit from a tee.

FACE
The hitting surface
(where the grooves are)
of a clubhead.

FADE
A shot which, for a right-handed player, purposely
drifts in a controlled fashion from left to right.
The opposite for lefties.

CLUBHOUSE CHATTER: HIGHEST SCORE ON A SINGLE HOLE IN A PGA TOURNAMENT

At the 1938 U.S. Open, Ray Ainsley, a pro from Ojai, California, recorded a score of 19 on the par-4 16th hole at Cherry Hills Country Club in Englewood, Colorado. Instead of taking a penalty drop when he sent his approach shot into a creek that bordered the green, Ainsley kept swinging away at the ball.

For almost half an hour he desperately tried to free his ball from the running water. Later, USGA Rules Committee Chairman Morton Bogue asked Ainsley why he hadn't just taken a drop.

"I thought I had to play the ball as it lay all the time," Ainsley replied. Then he recalled the rule allowing relief from a water hazard, in this case a flowing stream. Bud McKinney, his fellow competitor, remembered that day years later. "It was so funny watching him swipe at the ball. By the count of nine strokes, R. L. Anderson, the scorekeeper, started laughing so hard he fell down. Anderson said to me, 'I can't take this any longer, you take up the count.' I walked down the creek behind Ainsley and by this time, a couple of hundred people came down to see what was going on. Ainsley was hitting and hitting the ball and it would occasionally jump like a fish and land on the bank only to roll back in. The crowd would scream, 'There it is!' and then it would roll back into the water. At one point I remember Ainsley dropped a club in the water because the grip was so wet." He ended up losing almost 75 yards as the current pushed the ball downstream. Some people in the gallery disputed Ainsley's final score, thinking he made a 21 or even a 23. McKinney gave his total score as 19, and Ainsley posted a 96 for the round. Not surprisingly, he didn't win the tournament.

CLUBHOUSE CHATTER: PLAYERS' NICKNAMES

THE GOLDEN BEAR: An Australian sportswriter gave Jack Nicklaus the name in the early '60s because Nicklaus was large and blond. Nicklaus also attended a school as a kid where the mascots were the Golden Bears.

BUFFALO BILL: Billy Casper, winner of tournaments in the '50s, '60s, and early '70s, including two U.S. Opens and a Masters, was always battling his weight. He ate organic vegetables and buffalo meat, which helped keep his weight down and earned him his nickname.

FUZZY: Frank Urban Zoeller won the Masters at his first appearance at the event. He won many other PGA events. His nickname comes from his initials.

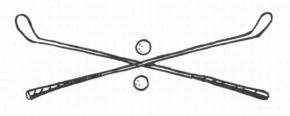

FAIRWAY

The areas of mown grass found between the tees, greens, and rough.

FAT SHOT

Hitting the turf before making contact with the ball.

FLOP SHOT

A type of chip hit high into the air so the ball will stop quickly on the green. **A Lob.**

FOOT WEDGE

When a player illegally kicks his ball into a better position. Not necessarily a shoe-in.

FORE

Loud shout warning nearby people that the ball might hit them. Derives from the cannon cry when bystanders were told to clear the fore prior to discharge.

FOOT WEDGE

FORECADDIE

FORECADDIE

A caddie who doesn't carry a bag, but tracks down balls, offers yardages, rakes bunkers, and reads greens.

FORWARD PRESS

A slight move of the hands toward the target before making a swing or a stroke.

GET LEGS

A term used by golfers to encourage the ball to travel in the air and/or roll when they think the shot is short.

GIMME

In casual golf, a very short putt that the other players agree can count automatically without actually being played. Contraction of the phrase "give me." **Tap-In.**

GOLDIE BOUNCE

When the ball hits a tree deep in the rough and bounces out onto the fairway.

CLUBHOUSE CHATTER: HIGHEST SCORE IN A BRITISH OPEN

Maurice Flitcroft, a British crane operator, crashed the qualifying rounds of the 1976 British Open by discovering a loophole on the application form: Amateurs, but not professionals, were required to enter their handicap on the form. Flitcroft sidestepped the issue by ticking off the box marked "professional." Dressed in plastic shoes and a fishing hat and never having played a full round of golf, he scored a 121, leading the press to refer to him as "British Open Chump."

Subsequently Flitcroft was effectively banned from every golf course in the country. However, years later he attempted to enter the Open, and several other golf competitions, either under his own name or under pseudonyms such as Gene Paceky (as in paycheck), Gerald Hoppy, Arnold Palmtree, and James Beau Jolley. At first he avoided detection by wearing various disguises: a large handlebar moustache and bizarre hats. But irate officials usually chased him off the course once they witnessed his incompetent playing.

CLUBHOUSE CHATTER: PLAYERS' NICKNAMES

THE GIANT: Standing six feet eight inches tall, Craig Smith is the tallest professional golfer in the world.

GREAT WHITE SHARK: His blond hair, six-foot frame, aggressive playing style, and birthplace in Australia, home to the shark, all contribute to Greg Norman's nickname. In the '80s and '90s he was considered the number one golfer for 331 weeks.

BABE: Mildred Ella Didrickson Zaharias, America's first female golf celebrity and leading player of the '40s, winning every golf title available by 1950. She became the first and only female golfer to make the cut at a PGA tour event, shooting 76 and 81 during the first two rounds of the 1945 Los Angeles Open. She says she got her nickname when she hit five homers in a childhood baseball game. She was compared to Babe Ruth, who was then in his heyday.

GREENIE

Hitting the green with a tee shot on a par 3.

GROUND UNDER REPAIR

An area of the golf course under construction marked by white dotted lines. Players can pick up the ball that lands there and move it to another area on the fairway without penalty.

HACKER

Poor player. Derives from the image of a player who swings wildly and digs up the turf.
A Duffer. A Chopper.

GROUND UNDER REPAIR

CLUBHOUSE CHATTER: HELL HOLES

Kip Henley was caddying for Brian Gay at the
RBC Heritage Tournament in 2012 at Harbour
Town Golf Links in Hilton Head Island, South
Carolina, when Gay's ball became stuck in the
mud on the fifteenth green. When Henley went
to free it, he encountered a six-foot-long alligator.
Henley calmly enlisted help from another caddie,
Scott Tway, and the two bopped the beast with a
rake until it sauntered away.

HANDSY

HAM AND EGG
When two players on a team pair well, with one player excelling whenever the other falters.

HANDICAP
A number assigned to each player based on his/ her ability, subtracted from the score at the end of a round. A way of providing equality among players of different abilities.

HANDSY
A player with too much wrist movement in his/ her swing or putting stroke, causing inconsistent shots or putts. **A Wristy.**

HARDPAN
Densely packed dirt or grass.

CLUBHOUSE CHATTER: AVIAN REFERENCES TO SCORES

The terms "birdie," "eagle," "albatross," and "condor" didn't originate simultaneously. It is widely believed that "birdie" was conceived at the Atlantic City Country Club in New Jersey in about 1903. William Smith hit a straight shot that landed close to the hole, which allowed him a short putt to score one under par. He exclaimed, "That was a bird of a shot!" (Bird in those days was American slang for something that was good.) Thereafter people at the club began to use the term "birdie" for a one-under-par score. The usage spread rapidly and by about 1913 the term was used in Scotland and in England, as well. "Eagle" was an American term, probably because the eagle, the American symbol, was clearly superior to a generic "bird." By about 1919, the term had reached golfers across the Atlantic. "Albatross," on the other hand, originated in Great Britain. Paradoxically, the word, usually associated with bad fortune, was used to describe a three-under-par score, because it is such a rare bird. American golfers more often use the term "double eagle," although it's not four under par (two plus two) but three.

An even rarer bird than an albatross is the condor, the largest flying bird in North America. In fact, scoring a "condor," a hole-in-one on a par 5, is virtually impossible and has only been recorded four times.

CLUBHOUSE CHATTER: PLAYERS' NICKNAMES

THE BLACK KNIGHT: South African legend, Gary Player, got his nickname because he is famous for wearing black, supposedly helping him absorb the sun's energy.

BOSS OF THE MOSS: Loren Roberts, known for his tremendous putting ability.

THE KING: Arnold Palmer, considered one of golf's greatest players.

SLAMMIN' SAMMY: Because top-notch golfer Sam Sneed hit the ball far.

HAZARD

A feature of a golf course intended to make play more difficult. The most common hazards are water, in the form of ponds or streams or bunkers: a hole or depression in the ground filled with sand.

HOLE

A round opening in the green (4.25 inches in diameter and at least four inches deep) that is the ultimate goal. The position of holes on the green is periodically changed. There are eighteen holes in a regulation golf course. **Can. Cup.**

THE HONOR

The privilege of hitting the first shot from the tee box. Typically earned by carding the lower score on the previous hole.

HAZARD

CLUBHOUSE CHATTER: HELL HOLES
A high-flying tee shot by golfer Dave Hickler, an airline executive, proved to be a bit fishy. In 1985 he was playing on the par 3 17th hole at Bangkok Country Club when his tee shot dropped in a water hazard – and then miraculously bounced out onto the bank. Hickler's shot had struck a 12-inch carp that was swimming near the surface of the water.

JUNK

HOSEL

The conduit that connects the shaft to the clubhead.

JUNK

Additional rewards added to a basic bet. For instance, two teams might agree to award a dollar for greenies and birdies. Can also mean rough or other difficult terrain. "I'm afraid that's in the junk."

KICK

The direction a ball bounces after landing.

LIE

How the ball sits on the ground after being hit. Determines the difficulty or the ease of the next stroke.

CLUBHOUSE CHATTER: MEN'S GOLF GARB

In the very earliest days of golf, players wore kilts and animal skins until Scottish aristocrats began taking in fresh air on the course. These golfers wore knickerbockers (knickers) and heavy tweed jackets—clothing to combat the wind blowing off of the ocean at courses like Saint Andrews in Scotland. Shirts with starched collars and neckties were also worn, along with sturdy shoes and tweed caps.

By the 1900s stylish golfers donned single-breasted jackets with a vest, then called a

waistcoat, and knickers, loose-fitting short pants, gathered at the knees. Long cotton "puttees" or stockings, a golf cap, and golf shoes completed the look.

As golf gained popularity among affluent players in the 1920s, they distinguished themselves by putting together formal outfits that included "plus fours" or knickers with four inches of extra length; patterned golf socks; and two-tone "spectator" shoes. Most golfers continued wearing a shirt and tie, and also donned knitted cardigans. On cooler days they wore "Norfolk" jackets, a loose, belted single-breasted jacket with box pleats in the back and front.

Golfers had replaced plus fours and knickers with pants in white and gray by the 1930s, since men sometimes went to the golf course straight from the office. However, many golfers stopped wearing neckties during this time.

The golf clothing worn today resembles outfits worn in the 1940s. Men wore short-sleeved knitted shirts and lightweight slacks. Sturdy shoes now had spiked soles, and hats had brims. For cooler weather, water-resistant "Eisenhower" jackets (named after President Eisenhower, a golfer) became popular. These jackets were more advantageous to the golf swing because of the generous shoulder fit and the snug waistband. Golfers also began to wear khakis or shorts with colorful shirts for warm weather, while cardigan sweaters continued to be popular for cooler days. By the early 1950s golf clothes were ablaze with color. A knitted golf shirt was matched with increasingly colorful pants and shirts. Arnold Palmer changed the look—now cotton shirts, lightweight tan pants and oxford shoes became the rage. By the 1960s and 1970s turtlenecks combined with colorful pants were popular. Houndstooth patterns, too, became a staple.

The slapstick comedy *Caddyshack* and the Reagan era influenced the return of more traditional clothing with a technological twist in the 1980s. Stretch fabrics, moisture-wicking shirts, and waterproof leathers became popular. By the 1990s designer attire and clothing with logo endorsements were the norm on the course.

The game of golf had changed into a more athletic event by 2000, and the apparel reflected that change. Today, clothing is designed for both high performance and high fashion. Male golfers normally wear knit collared "golf shirts" paired with roomy golf pants or shorts and a hat or a visor with a brim. For cool weather, golfers typically wear a vest, cardigan, or jacket. This clothing incorporates cutting-edge technology that continues to be perfected.

Always a sport that values good taste in fashion, golf has had several style icons over the years. Among them are Walter Hagen, Ben Hogan, and, of course, Arnold Palmer. But some pros have veered off course.

John Daly, who won the 1991 PGA Championship as an alternate, and then won the British Open four years later in 1995, is known for wearing lurid, super-loud clothes. His disco-designed pants, raspberry and yellow checked pants, and neon green hats make him hard to miss on the course.

Japanese golfer Shingo Katayama, the winner of twenty-seven Japanese tournaments, is known for wearing pink golfing gloves and a bright yellow cowboy hat on the course. Katayama, who tied for fourth place at the 2001 PGA Championship, is often called "Cowboy Shingo."

American golfer Rickie Fowler is known as the number one ranked golfer in the world for thirty-six weeks in 2007 and 2008. He's also well known for wearing all orange from head to toe during the final rounds of golf tournaments.

LIE ANGLE

Angle between the shaft and the heel of the clubhead.

LINKS

A type of golf course on the coast, originating in Great Britain. Characterized by sand, wind, few trees, and a rough of native grasses. The term is also used when referring to any golf course.

LOFT

Angle between the club's shaft and the club's face. Determines how high the ball will fly.

MATCHPLAY

Competition decided not by the best overall eighteen-hole score, but by the number of holes won, halved, or lost. A typical winning score in matchplay is 3 and 1, or three holes up with one hole to play.

MEMBER'S BOUNCE

A helpful bounce of the ball.

LIE ANGLE

CLUBHOUSE CHATTER: HELL HOLES

The ordinary-looking par 3 one-hole Camp Bonifas Golf Course, located in South Korea, is considered to be the most dangerous golf course in the world by *Sports Illustrated* magazine. A former UN command post, Camp Bonifas, located just south of the Korean Demilitarized Zone, is surrounded on three sides by landmines left over from the Korean War. Golfing equipment considered too dangerous to reclaim litters the edges of the green. Wayward balls have detonated at least one landmine.

MUDBALL

MUDBALL

A ball that has soil or debris stuck to it, affecting its flight.

MULLIGAN

A do-over, or replay of the shot, when playing a friendly round.

NASSAU

A tripartite bet originated in the 1900s at Nassau Country Club on Long Island, New York. Money is wagered on the front nine, the back nine, and the overall eighteen. Most popular bet in the game.

NINETEENTH HOLE

The bar at the clubhouse where players gather to have a drink and talk and swap lies.

NET

A player's score, adjusted by his/her handicap.

CLUBHOUSE CHATTER: WOMEN'S WEAR

The focus on women's golf attire was originally restrictive, with the attention on style, rather than practicality. In the 1800s women dressed for the game as if they were attending a tea party: bustles, crinolines, petticoats, and corsets were de rigueur, even if they impeded the ability to swing a club. By the early 1900s younger women began wearing a white blouse and long black skirt, topped by a boater, a fairly formal hat with a stiff, flat crown and brim. More elaborate hats were held in place by pins, and armbands held sleeves in place—

necessary measures so the ball could be seen when swinging a club.

In the 1920s, as women's street clothes became more practical, so did golf wear. Below-the-knee skirts coupled with sweaters were deemed suitable. However, in 1933, Gloria Minoprio, a six-foot-tall British golfer, pushed the boundaries. She arrived at the English Women's Championship at Westward Ho! Country Club in Sioux Falls, South Dakota, in a bright yellow chauffeur-driven Rolls Royce. When she appeared from the backseat of the car the crowd gasped. Minoprio's face had been whitened, her lips were painted a scarlet red, and she wore a close-fitting roll-neck sweater, kid gloves, a turban-like hat, and pants, or trousers as they were commonly called then. Not only was she the first woman golfer to wear pants, but her other claim to fame was winning the British women's golf championship using only one club (an equivalent of a 2-iron) during the entire tournament!

CLUBHOUSE CHATTER: PLAYERS' NICKNAMES

BAM-BAM: Brittany Lincicome: plays in Ladies Professional Golf Association (LPGA). She's one of the longest drivers in women's golf. Her exceptional length of tee has earned her her nickname.

LUMPY: Tim Herron's girth and open contempt for exercise and healthy foods earned him the nickname, which he's had since he was fifteen.

TIGER: Eldrick Woods's famous nickname was bestowed upon him as a child, when his father began calling him Tiger, as he called his friend in the military, a South Vietnamese lieutenant colonel. When Woods's father lost touch with the colonel after the war he said if he had another child (boy or girl) he would nickname him/her Tiger.

OPEN CLUBFACE

The clubface is pointed higher or to the right of the target at impact, causing the ball to fly high or right. The opposite for lefties.

OPEN STANCE

When the player is standing with his/her front foot pulled back from the ball, pointing left or right of the target.

PAR

Standard score for a particular hole.

PIN

A pole in the hole that holds a flag. Serves as an aiming aid.

PITCH-AND-RUN

A short shot not far from the green, using less than a full swing. Sends the ball with more accuracy than a full swing through with an iron.

OPEN STANCE

POP-UP

PITCH MARK

The dent that a golf ball makes when it lands on the green. **Ball Mark.**

POP-UP

When the top of the club head strikes under the ball, causing it to go straight up in the air. Not only are pop-ups bad shots, but also they often leave white scuffmarks on the top of the club-head. **Sky Shot.**

PRESS

A new bet typically proposed by the losing side. Some clubs play automatic.

PULL

For a right-handed golfer a shot that doesn't curve but lands considerably left of the hole. The ball will go in the opposite direction for a lefty.

CLUBHOUSE CHATTER: LONGEST SHOT

Here's a record that's out of this world. Before climbing aboard the Apollo 14 moon mission in 1971, Astronaut Alan Shepard brought the handle of a retractable instrument for collecting rock and soil samples to his friend, a Houston golf professional. Swearing him to secrecy, Shepard asked his friend to make a 6-iron club head fit on the handle of that instrument. The pro fulfilled his request and Shepard had his "golf club" to take with him in space. When Apollo 14 lifted off, only a handful of people knew of Shepard's plans to tee off on the moon. As the mission concluded, just before taking off, Shepard pulled out the club and two golf balls. He famously described his second shot as traveling "miles and miles," which was surely an exaggeration. Nevertheless, astrophysicists later calculated that a well-hit ball could have traveled over two miles. Shepard later joked that he played "winter rules in February" by improving his lie on the moon's surface.

PUNCH SHOT
A shot played low, often
to avoid overhead obstacles
or to compensate for high
winds. **Knockdown.**

PUSH
A shot that doesn't curve but lands significantly to
the right of the hole. Opposite for lefties.

PUTT
A precise shot on the green intended to roll the
ball into the hole.

PUTTER
A specialized, short, low-loft club designed
specifically for use on the green.

READING THE GREEN
When a player analyzes the dips and curves of
the green and length of its grass to determine the
speed and direction of his stroke.

READING THE GREEN

CLUBHOUSE CHATTER: GOLF TEES

In the early days of the game, golfers teed up on a small mound of moist sand. Caddies would dig sand out from the bottom of the holes to make the tees, which caused the holes to deteriorate. In the late 1800s golfers teed up the ball on small pieces of used cork, paper, or rubber until two members of the Tantallon Golf Club in England invented the earliest known portable golf tee in 1889. The small rubber slab rested flat on the ground with three vertical rubber prongs or a hollow rubber tube to hold the ball in place. Signaling the onset of golf tee technology wars, a few years later Englishman Percy Ellis patented

the very first tee to penetrate the ground, a rubber circle with a metal spike. The first United States patent for a golf tee, a rubber tee with a flat base and somewhat concave top, was issued to a Scot, David Dalziel, in 1896. P.M. Matthews of Scotland patented a variation of Ellis's tee, a cup-shaped rubber top connected to a ground spike in 1897. Two years later an American dentist, Dr. George F. Grant, one of the first African American graduates of Harvard and an avid golfer, patented a tee that he invented in 1898. A peg with a rubber top that was pushed into the ground, it was very close to the modern tee, without the concave head. But Grant was an inventor, not a marketer, and his invention wasn't widely accepted. It wasn't until 1921 that another American dentist, William Lowell, invented the first profitable tee. They were manufactured in wood and painted with red tops so they could easily be seen. He named it the "Reddy Tee," the one we know today. These tees were soon produced in a variety of styles and materials.

The "Reddy Tee" made of white celluloid by the Nieblo Manufacturing Company was patented in

1924. Although plastic tees are available, simple wooden tees similar to those made in the 1920s are still the most common type.

Up until 2004 when tee heights of no more than four inches were implemented in the USGA rules, there was no official height. Golfer Chi Chi Rodriguez, the first Puerto Rican to be inducted into the World Golf Hall of Fame, took advantage of this ruling and sometimes used a pencil on an extra long drive. At the 1979 U.S. Open he hollowed out the eraser section of his pencil with a divot tool and teed up. When playing golf in Puerto Rico as a poor youngster Rodriguez began using pencils as tees because tees were scarce. He once said, "The best wood in most amateurs' bags is a pencil."

ROUGH

ROUGH

Grass bordering the fairway, usually taller and coarser than the fairway.

SANDBAGGER

A golfer who has a higher handicap than his skills indicate. Viewed with disdain. **Bandit.**

SAND WEDGE

Lofted club with added "bounce" in the sole. Designed for play out of a bunker.

SANDY

When a golfer makes par after being in a bunker.

CLUBHOUSE CHATTER: GOLF BALLS THEN AND NOW

The first familiar form of golf was played with wooden balls, made of beech or box root. In 1618 a new type of ball consisting of a cowhide or horsehide sphere stuffed with goose or chicken feathers was introduced. These balls were made while the leather and feathers were still wet. As the leather shrank while drying, the feathers expanded to create a compact ball, which was

then painted white. This ball, expensive to make, had great flight features, but was easily damaged. It was used well into the nineteenth century, until 1848, when Rev. Dr. Robert Adams Paterson created a new ball. Called a "gutty," it was formed out of dried sap from the sapodilla tree, known as gutta-percha. Shaped into balls by heating up the sap and molding it while hot, the ball had a rubbery feel. The gutty, inexpensive to produce, transformed the game of golf, allowing it to spread far and wide. In the late 1890s golfers noticed that balls with rougher surfaces often flew straighter and farther than those with smooth exteriors. At first, the balls were hand hammered to produce the desired roughness. Later, dimples were incorporated into the molds. Not all golf balls have the same number of dimples, depending on which company designs the ball. Currently the ideal ball has between 380 and 432 dimples.

In the 1890s B.F. Goodrich Company introduced a ball with a center of tightly wound rubber bands. Wound balls went out of favor about a hundred years later and were replaced by solid core balls with better performance. Today, the creation of this small round object is constantly reaching new levels of closely guarded design, the result of leading edge technologies. Americans now spend approximately $600 million on golf balls every year.

SCRAMBLE

Make a good score from a trying location.
Seve Ballesteros. A Seve. Also a form of play, typically used in casual competitions featuring a wide spectrum of skill levels. Each player hits a shot. The group then votes on the best one and plays in from there in similar fashion.

SCRATCH

A handicap of zero. This means a player usually shoots around even par.

SHANK

The consequence of a ball coming into contact not with the clubface but with the hosel. The ball can travel in any direction, most often 90 degrees to the right for a right-handed player.

SIT

Telling the ball to drop softly and not to roll after landing. Similar to talking to your dog: Sit! Stay!

SHANK

CLUBHOUSE CHATTER: BRIEF HISTORY OF GOLF CLUBS

In golf's early days in Scotland, clubs were hand carved by players. Club heads were made of hard woods such as beech, apple, holly, and pear, while shafts were made from ash or hazel, softer woods, providing more flexibility. Eventually skilled craftsmen were employed to make the clubs. A set of clubs included play clubs (long-noses) for driving, fairway clubs (or grassed drivers) for medium-range shots, spoons for short-range shots, niblicks (similar to today's wedges), and a putting club. The clubs, especially long-noses and niblicks, broke often. In fact, golfers could expect to break at least one club during a round. Some club makers experimented with using leather, metal, and bone fragments in their club faces to prevent the club from shattering and consequently to improve distance.

Indeed, as early as 1750 some club makers used forged metal heads for niblicks. But, it wasn't until the introduction of the rubber gutta-percha ball in 1848 that golfers were no longer concerned with damaging the ball and started using clubs with iron heads. These heads could be molded with striking faces tilted in various degrees and were stronger than wood. Club heads of irons (naturally called irons) were used for making shorter, high-arc shots. Now, wooden-headed clubs (called woods) came to be used for making longer, low-trajectory shots. All clubs had wooden shafts, whether they had iron or wooden heads.

In the 1920s the first steel-shafted clubs were made in the United States. Around this time club manufacturers began using the current numbering system to classify the different clubs, instead of using their old names. Woods were numbered one through five and irons were numbered two through nine. The higher the number, the greater the loft provided by the striking face. The putter retained its name, instead of being assigned a number. In 1931 a new club was added: the sand wedge, helping golfers lift the ball out of sand traps.

In the 1970s manufacturers introduced fiber-reinforced composite materials for shafts that were originally developed for military and aerospace uses. In 1979 the first metal-headed drivers were introduced, followed in 1989 by significantly larger metal-headed drivers. The combination of improved shaft technology and larger club head allowed golfers to hit the ball farther.

Fourteen clubs are the maximum allowed in one player's golf bag during a round under the Rules of Golf. Any number below fourteen is fine. Those fourteen clubs can't be changed during the course of one round. But if a golfer begins with fewer than fourteen, he/she may add clubs during a round as long as they aren't borrowed from another player and no delay is caused.

SKULL

SKULL

Hitting the ball above its equator, causing it to skid on the ground.

SLICE

For a right-hander, a shot with a significant unintended left to right trajectory. The opposite for a leftie.

SNOWMAN

When a player takes eight shots to complete a hole. Known because of the shape of the number eight.

STINGER

A shot played low and hard. Made famous by Tiger Woods.

CLUBHOUSE CHATTER: QUEEN OF CLUBS

The slim, nearly six-foot-tall Mary, Queen of
Scots, was the first woman golfer, and is often
called the Mother of Golf. Having learned
to play as a princess raised in France where
military cadets carried the royal clubs, Mary
called her assistants "cadets," using the French
pronunciation cad-eh. She is often credited with
coining the term "caddie."

It was during Mary's reign that the famous golf
course at Saint Andrews was built in 1552. It is
said that she loved that course, where she kept a

small vacation cottage. Mary, granddaughter of James IV and mother of James VI of Scotland and I of England, was scorned by her political enemies for playing the game just days after her second husband, Henry Stuart, Lord Darnley, was strangled. George Buchanan, a Scottish historian and later Mary's tutor, consequently wrote that she had been playing sports that were clearly "unsuitable to women."

Mary was forced to flee England in 1568 when charges of murder were brought against her. Many of her accusers claimed that because she went on the golf course instead of mourning her husband she was surely guilty. She spent the rest of her life in prison and was not allowed any form of exercise.

When Queen Elizabeth ordered Mary's beheading in 1587, Mary's golf game once again came back to haunt her, with the rumor being that her early return to the course contributed to Queen Elizabeth's death sentence decision.

CLUBHOUSE CHATTER: PLAYERS' NICKNAMES

BIG MOMMA: Joanne Gunderson Carner, know as "Great Gundy," was to the women's tour what Jack Nicklaus was to the men's: a large hitter with a passion for the game. In the middle of winning her second U.S. Women's title in 1976, fellow golfer Sandra Palmer dubbed Carner "Big Momma," a nickname that stuck.

LEFTY: Phil Mickelson, one of sixteen golfers in the history of the sport to win at least three of the four professional majors, plays left-handed, though he is actually a righty. As a child he learned to play golf by mirroring his father's swing.

STROKE PLAY

Also known as medal play, this is the form of competition played on the PGA Tour. The winner plays the eighteen (or seventy-two) holes in the fewest strokes.

TEE

A wooden peg where a ball is placed for a drive. It can only be used in the tee box, used to improve a lie.

TEE BOX

Area at the beginning of the hole where the ball is placed, between the markers, and the game is started.

TEXAS WEDGE

The use of the putter from off the green as opposed to a traditional chipping club.

TEXAS WEDGE

TURKEY

THIN
Hitting the ball a little low on the clubface, causing a low trajectory with poor distance control.

TIPS
The set of tees from which the course plays the longest. A golfer starting here is said to be "playing the tips." **Back Tees, Championship Tees.**

TURKEY
Three birdies, one after another, in a single round of golf. Reason for giving thanks!

VELCRO
Greens that are slow. The ball sticks to the green.

WAGGLE
A player's adjustments to his body and the club prior to swinging. It can be a nervous habit or intentional.

CLUBHOUSE CHATTER: HOLE-IN-ONE

There's a lot of luck in hitting a hole in one, no matter how you slice it. Children as young as five years old have achieved it, and so has a 103-year-old man. Additionally, many famous non-professional golfers have had a bit of good fortune on the golf course over the years. Baseball Hall of Fame catcher Carlton Fisk hit his to win a Lexus on the 155-yard, par-3 fourteenth hole at TPC Summerlin, an eighteen-hole championship golf course in Las Vegas, in the 1998 Robert Gamez Celebrity Classic. Fisk used an 8-iron.

Former Major League Baseball pitcher Roger Clemens wasn't just an ace on the mound. He made his fifth golf ace at the Bob Hope Chrysler Classic in January 2006, which helped him and

actor Matthew McConaughey win the celebrity tournament.

Three U.S. presidents, all Republicans, have recorded aces: Gerald Ford, Dwight Eisenhower, and Richard Nixon. With a 5-iron Nixon hit his ace at Bel Air Country Club in 1961. He said, "It was the greatest thrill in my life — even better than being elected." He was referring to his Senate election, since he wasn't elected President of the United States until seven years later.

To date there has only been a single hole-in-one on a par-4 hole in a PGA tournament, and an unconventional one at that. It occurred in 2001 at TPC Scottsdale, home of the Phoenix Open, then called the FBR Open. Andrew Magee, just an average driver of the ball, didn't think he could reach the green on hole 17, measuring 332 yards from the tee to the green. Instead of waiting for the group ahead to clear the green, he teed up and swung. He was shocked when his ball went so far that it ran up onto the green, where a group was still putting. One of the players was squatting, studying the line of his putt, and didn't notice the ball coming. Magee's ball traveled through the player's legs, ricocheted off his putter, and dropped right into the cup. There was no controversy as to whether Magee's ace broke any rules because it was deemed that he accidentally hit the putter. He would have been penalized if his shot hit the golfer or his caddie.

There's a long-standing tradition for any golfer who makes an ace. The lucky golfer is required to buy drinks in the clubhouse after the round for anyone playing in the same group and for anyone else who witnessed the hole-in-one. Although this tradition has no basis in any rulebook, one round of drinks is expected, and anything beyond that is up to the player. Some more generous golfers will end up buying several rounds of drinks, or even a round for everyone in the clubhouse, after making a hole-in-one.

Many golfers buy hole-in-one insurance to cover the cost of drinks. In Japan the insurance is particularly worthwhile as golfers who hit an ace are expected to buy gifts or even throw a party in addition to buying a round of drinks.

WATERY GRAVE

A final resting place for a miss-hit shot into a water hazard. RIP.

WINTER RULES

Allows ball to be cleaned and moved because of poor condition of the course.

WORMBURNER

A ball, typically topped or thinned, that skims the surface.

YIPS

When a player has a tendency to twitch during the putting stroke. Can also occur during chips and even full swings. **Twitches. Staggers. Jitters. Jerks. Jumps. Shakes. Flinches.**

WATERY GRAVE

CLUBHOUSE CHATTER: MIDNIGHT GOLF

A game of midnight golf seems like a preposterous idea. But not in Iceland, which boasts more golf courses per person than any other country. During the summer solstice, professionals and amateurs alike tee off at midnight at Akureyri Golf Club—the most northerly eighteen-hole golf course on earth. The tournament, the biggest in Iceland, is played over two late nights—more accurately early mornings—on the spectacular course surrounded by lava fields.

More adventurous golfers can participate in the Arctic Open held in winter. This one is played with black golf balls, spotted more easily in the snow.

ZINGER

ZINGER
A ball hit high and hard.

ABOUT THE AUTHORS

SALLY COOK

Sally Cook is the author, with James Charlton, of *How to Speak Baseball* and *Hey Batta Batta Swing! The Wild Old Days of Baseball,* illustrated by Ross MacDonald. She coauthored, with legendary football coach Gene Stallings, *Another Season: A Coach's Story of Raising an Exceptional Son,* a *New York Times* bestseller.

ROSS MACDONALD

Ross MacDonald's illustrations have appeared in *The New York Times, The New Yorker, Rolling Stone, Harper's, The Atlantic Monthly,* and *Vanity Fair.* He has also written and illustrated several books for children and adults. His most recent is *What Would Jesus Craft?*